The Battle of the Books of Jonathan Swift: Literary and critically analysis in cultural aspect

Dr. Prohlad Roy

The Battle of the Books of Jonathan Swift: Literary and critically analysis in cultural aspect

Laxmi Book Publication
Solapur, Maharastra

The Battle of the Books of Jonathan Swift: Literary and critically analysis in cultural aspect

Publisher: Dr. A. Yakkaldevi, Founder & Executive Editor
Laxmi Book Publication
Solapur, Maharastra
Laxmi Book Publication
258/34, Raviwar Peth, Solapur-413005, Maharashtra, India.
Phone :
+91-9595 359 435 (Mob.)
0217-2372010 (Office)
Email :
ayisrj@yahoo.in
ayisrj2011@gmail.com
aygrt@yahoo.com

Printed in India
First published, 2014
Price Rs. 200

ISBN

Cover Design: @LBP
Available at:

- 258/34 , Raviwar Peth,Solapur-413 005,Maharashtra, India.
- Dr. Prohlad Roy, Simantapalli, Santiniketan, Birbhum, West Bengal
- Mr. Ashim Kumar Roy, Kuntighat, Bishpara, Nayasharai, Hooghly, W.B.

Preface

Contents

Literature and Social atmosphere
The Peculiarity of Swift
Swift's Plea
A story teller
Life and Works of Jonathan Swift (1667-1745)
"Swift is clear but shallow
The Champion of Reason in Style
Swift's own views
Ironical Vision
Satiric Prose
The Prose Style
Theme, as proposed by Swift
Cazamian rightly remarks

Bibliography

Literature and Social atmosphere

Literature, in the age of Swift was essentially the literature of the town, born in town, written for the town, and often portraying the life of the town to the minutest detail. The London of Swift is even more wonderfully alive to us through literature that the London of Shakespeare. We can see its ill-paved streets with their narrow sidewalks and their running gutters; we know Grub Street where obscure authors fought with debts and starvation; the Fleet; the gay boating party on the Thames; the pleasure-gards where society drank and flirted, listened the music, and exclaimed at the fireworks. All that restless, gay, animated life is still before us; the beauty in her sedan chair; the beau with his lace ruffles and his flowing wig; and we can imagine the courtly presentation of the snuff-box, or the flutters of the fan. But this brilliant surface was but a thin viner, and beneath it life was vulgar, vicious and cruel.

The age which prided itself on its polish and politeness indulged in bull-baiting and cock-fights; its young aristocrats, wondering in drunken frolics through the ill-lighted London streets, habitually committed the most shocking outrages on unoffending passengers. Drunkenness, says a high authority, "became for the first time a national vice." It was confined to no class of society, and there is hardly an author of the so-called Augustan Age who was entirely free it. Its underlying brutality and coarseness of thought and action stain the pages of its literature; its misanthropy, its petty spites, and literary rivalries, break out in slanderous abuse, and bitter, mirthless satires. On every side are indications of a low moral tone. At the beginning of the century the Church was lifeless and worldly, and its great places were intrigued for and sought after as political spoil. Public life was debased, and bribery was regarded as a regular feature in the conduct of government. Many of the greatest man of the time, disgusted with the mercenary spirit and low aims which surrounded them, lost confidence in human virtue, and expressed sometimes with terrible power- their cynical contempt for man, and their hatred of his pate world. Yet even at this time the higher and nobles elements of the English character were struggling to reassert themselves, and long before the death of Pope, the spiritual redemption of England had begun.

The age of Pope, Dryden and Swift is called the Classical Age of the Augustan Age. It is called the Classical Age because the writers of this Age believed in and followed the models and literary standards of the classical Latin writers of the past. It was called the Augustan Age because they considered the England of that time the golden age of English literature like the Age of Augusts of the golden age of Latin literature.

The word 'classic', in relation to literature is defined by Sainte Beuve as what is very good and is made to last. The Oxford English Dictionary defines it as (1) one of the first class, of the highest rank or importance; approved as a model; standard, leading. (2) Of or belonging to the standard authors of the Greek and Latin antiquity. (3) In the style of the literature of the Greek and Latin antiquity.

In English literature, Classicism is usually regarded as a quality of the Augustan Age which affected a great admiration of the ancients and a rigid code of critical values and literary forms. The artificialities of the period, however as exemplified, for example, in Pope's translation from Homer make the comparison true as regards aim rather than achievement. The term is used mainly by way of contrast with the Romantic Age which followed.

Augustan Age is a period of literary eminence in the life of a nation, so named because during the reign of the emperor Augustus (27 B. C. – A. D. 14) Virgil, Horace, Ovid, Tibullus, & C., flourished. The term is usually applied in the history of English literature to the period of Pope and Addison. Among other famous writers of the time were Steele, Swift, Defoe, Gay, Prior and Congreve. It was notable for the perfection of the heroic couplet and the development of a clear logical prose style. Some of these characteristics are to be found in time of Dryden, but the Elizabethan qualities of rhetoric and eloquences in prose, conceit and bombast in verse still remained.

The Augustan Age had a classical evenness, a preference for wit and elegance, and for intellectual rather than emotional satisfaction. Its traditions survived throughout the greater part of the 18th century, notably in the writings of Johnson, Goldsmith, and Sheridan.

For a detailed study Goldsmith's Augustans Age in England; Saintsbury's Peace of the Augustans and Austin Dobson's Eighteenth Century Vignettes may be consulted. In French literature the term is applied to the period of Corneille, Racine, and Moliere.

The history of the early part of the eighteenth century shows a continuation of the social and literary forces which had begun with the Restoration. It was a period in which imagination slept, and in which the sense of the temporal realities of life was strong. It was a period of criticism rather than of creation, a period in which regularity and perfection of literary form were of more importance than originality of thought. It was an age of interest in the development of society and of institutions, rather than in the assertion of the individual. In particular, indeed, it went beyond the Restoration period.

The literature, especially drama, of this latter epoch was marked by something of the license of the Renaissance. The protest of Jeremy Collier against the stage, in 1698, was typical of the attitude of the new century, which realized and feared the anti-social effect of vice. These tendencies towards realizing of subject-matter, towards technical perfection of form, and toward social usefulness of purpose, are notably illustrated by the three chief figures of the literature of the age of Queen Anne – Swift, Addison and Pope.

Jonathan Swift's writings were occasional, and grew out of the circumstance of his life. Among his merits as a writer is his clearness. Further his contempt for all kinds of sham led him to despise literary affectation, directness and simplicity are the virtues by which he sets most store. His style is too severe, too sternly practical, too reserved, too dry. It presents men and things in too hard a light, with too sharp an outline, without the softening and colour which come from a sympathetic temperament. Absolute, unmitigated prose he wrote – the quintessence prose.

Joseph Addison cared for the literary cultivation of his readers. He made a novel contribution to literature in a series of sketches of character and contemporary types – of himself as the Spectator, of Sir Andrew Freeport, the merchant of Sir Roger de Coverley, the country gentleman, of Will Honeycomb the main of fashion. Dr. Johnson wrote of him, "Whoever wishes to attain an English style, familiar but not coarse, and elegant but not ostentatious, must give his days and nights to the volumes of Addison."

Pope owed his success to his marvelous skill in handing the heroic couplet. He declares that as a child he lisped in numbers, for the numbers came. But he was not satisfied with precocious amateurism. One of his earliest friends and critics, William Walsh, pointed out to him that "though we had several great poets, we never had any one great poet that was correct." Correctness accordingly, Pope made his aim from the first. Correctness requires patience, and genius for taking pains, Pope had in abundance. Nor did he sacrifice to mere exactness of metre and rhyme the other virtues of couplet verse, compression, epigrammatic force, and brilliancy of diction. Still, it is not to be wondered at that, in the long process of polishing and revising to suit a standard of extreme nicely, he lost something of the spontaneity of his first attempts.

The Peculiarity of Swift

Swift is the friend of Pope and Addison. Pope has satirized the whims and phantasm of society. To him the lock is enriched in the stars. The billet-deux is the most important feature for the feminine grace. To Swift the thing is different. In the Gulliver's Travels, he paints men as small as Thumb and as great as the pinnacle, meaning thereby there are persons as meek as the former as proud as the latter. In the Tale of the Tub, he points out what wrong conceptions are maturing in the field of religion. In the Battle of the Books, he has, a new theme to proclaim – The murderers think themselves more wise than the ancients. Dryden thinks him superior to Virgil and Bentley above all."

The satire, according to Swift, is a sort of glass, where in beholders do generally discover every body's face but their own, which is the chief reason for that kind of reception it meets in the world, and that so very few are offended with it.

To Swift, satire may be a glass but it is the reflexion of the innerself. People satirize when they are unable to fulfill that field of life which they are not capable of. Swift wrote first unanimously. Why? In order to conceal his identity. Why? He feared he might not be offended and oppressed by his antagonists. It may be true he was sincere, impartial and just but the just does not care for the approach of death. A true Christian must court charon, as Jesus lively did. Why did he then try to obscure himself?

Swift's Plea

The danger (Of Writing Satire) is not great, and has learned from long experience, never to apprehend mischief from those understandings, I have been able to provoke! For anger and fury though they add strength to the sinews of the body, yet are found to relax those of the mind, and render all its efforts feeble and impotent.

To comment upon this fact, it sounds reasonable what Dryden said of him, "Cousin, You cannot write poetry," and so Swift turned to prose and while writing prose, he had in his mind his own disappointment of love with his own beloved, his not reputing public, but like Chaucer he could not be popular. He has the germs of a propagandist but he had to die a sad death. A hungryman knows no harm in throwing stones upon the other. Swift is great in as much as his style is concerned, as regards the irony, he is not.

A story teller

As Robinson Crusoe is greatly admired, as Don Quixote is much appreciated, so is the case with the Gulliver's Travels. Swift is the master of style. His imagination has taken the reins in this book. He criticizes the psychology of the upper class, of the politicians, of the dandies and he says.

There is a brain that will endure but one scrumming. Let the owner gather it with discretion, and manage his little stock with husbandry; but of all things, let him beware of bringing it under the last of his betters; because that will make it all bubble up into impertinence, and he will find no new supply. Wit without knowledge, being a sort of cream, which gathers into a night to the top, and by a skilful hand, may be soon whip into forth, but once scrummed away, what appears underneath will be fit for nothing, but to be thrown to hogs.

It should be remembered that there is a difference between mind and the brain. The brain is a physiological organ; it can be replaced. Mind is the activity personified. A man may possess the brain of a dog but if his mind is regular he will rule over the realm of the hemisphere. We can make hell a heaven, and heaven a hell.

In the century, Swift lived, however he has quoted many illustrious names of the ancients and the moderns – Homer, Virgil, Pindar, Descartes and Wotton, Dryden, Bentley, - but he seems to be ignorant of their full text. The philosophy of man requires complete understanding of the soul. He fears to identify men and so the book – seller's comment reads : I must warn the reader, to beware of applying to persons what is here meant, only of books in the most literal sense. So, when Virgil is mentioned, we are not to understand the Person of a famous poet, called by that name, but only certain sheets of paper bound up in leather, containing in print, the works of the said poet, and so of the rest.

To sum up, Swift is swift in his satire, in the arguments and in his style. Like Browne his style is not turf, like Milton it is not pedantic, like Bacon it is not epigrammatic, but like many it is all in itself.

Life and Works of Jonathan Swift (1667-1745)

Swift, Jonathan (1667-1745), was a cousin of Dryden, and was educated at Kikenny Grammar School, where Congreve was his school-fellow. He was admitted (1689) to the household of sir W. Temple, where he acted as secretary. He wrote Pindarics, one of which provoked, according to Dr. Johnson, Dryden's remark, 'Cousin Swift you will never be a poet'. He returned to Ireland, was ordained (1694), but came back to Temple in 1696, when he edited Temple's correspondence, and in 1697 wrote the 'The Battle of the Books,' which was published in 1704, together with 'A Tale of a Tub,' his celebrated satire on 'corruption in religion and learning.' At Moor Park he first met Esther Johnson (Stella). On the death of Temple 1699, Swift went again to Ireland, and was given a rebind in St. Patrick's Dublin. In the course of numerous visits to London he becomes acquainted with Addison, Steele, Congreve, and Halifax. He began in 1708 a series of pamphlets on church questions with his ironical 'Argument against abolishing Christianity.' Amid these serious occupations, he diverted himself with the series of squibs upon the astrologer John Partidge (1707-9), and his poems, depicting scenes of London life, which were published in the 'Talter' (1709). Disgusted at the Whig alliance with dissent he went over to the Tories in 1710, attached the Whigminster in the 'Examiner,' which he edited, and in 1711 wrote 'The Conduct of the Allies' and some Remarks on the Barrier Treaty,' pamphlets written to dispose the mind of the nation to peace. He became dean of St. Patrick's in 1713. He had already begun his 'Journal to Stella,' which is a series of intimate letters (1710-13) to Esther Johnson and her companion Rebecca Dingley, for the most part written in babylanguage recounting the details of his daily life while in London. Swift's relations with Stella have remained somewhat obscure; she was his worshipper, and he respected her and returned her affection. Whether he ultimately married her is uncertain. Stella died in 1728. Another woman, Esther Vanhomrigh, entered into his life in 1708; she fell deeply in love with him, received some measure of encouragement, and his final rupture with her about 1723 led to her death. The story of their love-affair is related in Swift's poem, 'Cadenus and Vanessa.' In 1714 he joined Pope, Arbuthnot, Gay, and others in the celebrated Scriblerus Club. He returned to lreland in August 1714 and by his famous 'Drapier's Letters' (1724) he prevented the introduction of 'Wood's Half-pence' into lreland. He published 'Gulliver's Travels' in 1726, and paid a last visit to England in 1727. He kept up his correspondence with Bolingbroke. Pope, gay, or Arbuthnot, attacted to himself a small circle of friends, and was adored by the people. For a time before his death he was insane. He was buried by the side of Stella, in St. Patrick's Dublin, his own famous epitaph, 'ubisaeva indignation ulterius cor lacerare nequit,' being inscribed on his tomb. His indignation at oppression and unfairness was genuine. His writing was sometimes course, but never lewd. His political works are founded on common sense, and he had not party bias. Nearly all his works were published anonymously and for only one, 'Gulliver's travel', did he receive any payment.

War is the product of pride and pride is the outcome of Riches. People believe that was is really the child of pride. But very few accept. Pride as the daughter of riches. Pride is akin to beggary and want of something. In case everybody is well-to-do, there is no question of pride. A conflict always issues forth between poverty and plenty. Lust and avarice a4re the most ancient natural grounds of quarrel. They are certainly the issues of want. When people are hungry, they quarrel like dogs. Quarrelling on petty matters is found among ladies. Jealousy and suspicion makes people quarrel. Only of more courage, conduct or fortune wins the laurels.

The ancient and modern authors were seen in conflict. The moderns asked the ancients to leave that top of the hill or lower it down. The Ancients did not agree. In this war large quantities of ink were consumed and violence of both parties went on increasing. Their attacks were known as disputes, arguments, rejoinders, brief considerations, answers, remarks, reflections, objection and refutations, answers, remarks, reflections, objection and refutations. Books containing such attacks were known as Books of controversy.

In the Books controversy, we find preserved the spirit of each warrior (each learned writer). These books are generally kept in a separate part of the library. They are kept bound to one another with strong iron chains so that they may not use violence against one another. The books written by Scouts were combined with the books by his master Aristotle. Both these kinds of books made a joint attack upon the books written by Plato. The attack proved successful. Plato who had enjoyed the supreme position for about eight centuries found himself displaced by his attackers.

The public peace of the libraries must never have been broken, had they been bound to peace with strong iron chains. If it is not done, there will remain fear of the conflict and war. Swift points out that, when the books were admitted first into the public libraries, he was sure that they would create broils. People did not believe him then. He advised that the champions of each side should not be coupled together or intermingled in a way that their ill will might not poison the current of healthy stream of life. At that time nobody believed to his advice which came to be true seeing the fight that happened on Friday last between the Ancient and Modern Books in the James's Library. It was the reason that he had resolved to write down a full impartial account thereof.

Swift launches his personal attacks on some of the modern critics and innovators. He singles out Richard Bentley who pretended him to have been greatly zealous on behalf of the moderns. He usurped his erudition 'to knock down two of the Ancient chiefs'. As a result all books began to be kept by the moderns in the best places and books of the Ancients in the obscure corners. A strange confusion now began to appear. It was result of this mental confusion that now the books of modern and ancient authors now lay on the shelves mingled together.

The moderns tried to supersede the Ancients. One of the moderns made a four of the whole library to know the number and strength of their supporters. The moderns were informed that they were fully prepared and armed. In the midst of excitement and mutual suspicion hot words were exchanged between the moderns and Ancients. A spirit of active hostility now showed it self on both sides. One of the authors of the Ancient times offered to arbitrate in the dispute. He claimed that ancients possessed high merits. The moderns refused to believe that they owed any debt to the Ancients. Plato laughed at the foolish claims made by the moderns.

William temple heard the moderns. He informed the Ancients. Several of the moderns joined the Ancients. Temple had been educated among the Ancients for a long time. Though he was Modern, he joined the Ancients and became their greatest champion.

Swift describes the dispute between a spider (Moderns) and a Bee (Ancients) upon the highest corner of a large window, there lived a certain spider. Into the spider's web flies a Bee who extricates unharmed and pauses at a safe distance to clean his wings. The spider whose web has been ruined, spies the culprit, and shouts insults at him. He calls him a rascal, a vagabond without house or home, universal plunderer of nature. To which the Bel assures to come near his venal no more. He asks him to have patience. The spider again calls him rogue and advises him to respect his betters. The bee asks the spider why he thinks him superior to the Bee.

The spider curses the Bee. He is born to no possession of his own except a pair of wings and a drone-pipe. He is a plunderer and he steals honey from the garden whereas he (the spider) has been furnished with a native stock. He has his own castle to live in. he is rather a technician, a scientist than a foolish philosopher, indulged in thinking and thinking. The Bee says that he (spider) dwells in a narrow space and feeds upon his own poison. He turns everything into poison by his excessive pride. He produces nothing useful.

This dispute between the Bee and the spider (The Ancients and the Moderns) could not be fully decided. For sometimes both the parties remained silent. The Bee grew impatient at so much loss of time. He fled straight to a bed of Roses without looking for a reply and left the spider to weave his own cowed and mutter what he wanted.

Aesop sums up the dispute. The spider with his love of dirt and his self sufficiency is a perfect is a perfect modern, whereas the bee lives as do the Ancients bringing home honey and wax and thus furnishing which are sweetness and light. Instead of dirt and poison Bee chooses to fill Hives with Honey and Wax and thus furnishing mankind with the two noblest of things, which are sweetness and light.

Swift gives a mock description of the actual 'Battle of the Books.' He describes both well-armed parties. Their 'Heavy Cavalry' stands for epic and serious poetry. The ' Light House' stands for lyric and less serious composition. The moderns wrangle about the choice of leader because every private trooper pretends to be the chief, command from Tasso and Milton to Dryden and Wither. The Moderns are more numerous and more mutinous whereas the Ancients accept Hower as leader. They are more disciplined.

Here is given the list of the combatants

For the Ancients –

1. Homer (9th century B.C.), the greatest epic poet author of Illiad and odyssey.
2. Pindar (522-442 B.C.) famous Greek lyric poet, especially foe Odes.
3. Plato (427-347B.C.) the most famous name in Philosophy, disciple of Socrates.
4. Aristotle (384-322B.C.) great critic and thinker.
5. Herodotus (490-425B.C.) Historian.
6. Livy (49-17A.C.) Roman Historian.
7. Hippocrates (460-357B.C.) Famous Greek Physician.
8. Vossius (Gerard John) (1577-1640) Dutch poet.
9. Temple, Sir William, Swift's patron (1628-1699)

For the Moderns –

1. Milton (1606-1674) English Epic Poet.

2. Despreaux or Boilean, French Critic (1636-1711)
3. Cowley, Abraham (1618-1667)
4. Hobbes, Thomas (1588-1679)
5. Descartes, Reve (1596-1679) French Philosopher of the Seventeenth Century.

The actual encounter of the two belligerent groups and several single combats between the champions is –

1. Dryden Vs. Virgil
2. Cowley Vs. Pindar
3. Aristole Vs. Bacon.
4. Boyle Vs. Bentley and Wotton.

In the Milky Way the gods convened in council to watch the momentous battle now in progress on the library shelves. Fame went to Jupiter. She delivered a faithful account of all that passed between the two sides. Momus, patron god of the moderns, made an excellent speech in favour of the moderns. It was answered by Pallas, the protected of the Ancients. Jupiter commanded that the Book of Fate must be brought it at once. It had three large volumes containing the incidents of the past, present and future. Jupiter read it. At first be decided to convey to them his judgment but after reading the book silently, he shut up the book and spoke nothing.

The senate house was without the doors. So a large number of light, nimble gods and menial servants of Jupiter entered there. They used to receive and deliver the message by and to Jupiter. Jupiter gave them some message and commanded them to fly down to the library where they flew away and after pausing for a while, they entered the library unseen. These deities are called by mortal men as Accidents or Events but the gods call them second causes.

Momus feared lest worse should happen to the moderns. He ran hurried by to a malignant deity called criticism. She lived on the top of a snowy mountain in Nora Zembla. There lay spoils of numberless works of the writers. At her right sat her husband and father named ignorance at her left pride her mother. There was opinion, her sister. About her played her children, Noise and Impudence, Dullness and vanity, postiveness, pedantry, and Ill-manners. Momus requested criticism not to remain sitting there. She should go to the library where a battle between the Ancients and the moderns was waging. He requested her to haste to prevent their destruction. Momus left the goddess to her own will and went away. Criticism rose up and felt angry. She asked her family members to accompany her to the British Isle. She sat in her chariot with her parents, her sister and children and reached the fatal plain of St. James's Library at the time when the two parties were going to fight.

Criticism's attention was drawn towards the troop of modern Bow-men. She cast her eyes upon Wotton. She went to Bentley, Wotton's dearest friend. She asked Wotton not to sit idle. She took the ugliest of her monsters from her spleen and flung it into Wotton's mouth. She ordered two of her children, Dulness and Ill-manners to attend his person closely. Then she vanished.

Swift describes the battle in an epic way. He requests the goddess that presides over History, who he was that first advanced in the field of battle. Parcelsus darted his javelin with a mighty force which the Ancient Galen received upon his shield and the point of the javelin got broken. They took away the wounded Parcelsus to his chariot.

Aristotle draws his bow to the head and Pet flies his arrow at Bacon but it hits Descartes, and kills him. Homer tramples Dowenant. At first he advances against Gondibert whom he overthrows, horse and man to the ground. Then he slays Denhan, a stout Modern.

Then Virgil appears on the left wing of the horse, clad in shining armor. He cast his eyes to and fro and attacks Dryden. Dryden calls him 'Father' and Virgil spares his life. They exchange their armor.

Lucan appears upon a fiery horse of admirable shape. He makes a mighty slaughter. Blackmone, a famous modern, tries to oppose him. He darts a javelin which strikes deep in the earth. Then Lucan throws a lance but Aesculapius turns off the point. Lucan thinks that some god protects him. They decide to fight no longer. The goddess Dulness tames an Ogleby, by whom he is disarmed and assigned to his repose.

The battle still continues. Pindar does not follow one direction but moves on and on. He makes a terrible slaughter of the moderns. Cowley marches against Pindar. He throws a lance which misses Pindar and falls down. Then Pindar darts a javelin. Cowley is luckily saved by the shield of Venus. Then they draw swords. Pindar cuts down the modern into two.

Bentley is seen. He reaches where the modern chiefs are holding a meeting. He asks them to march against the Ancients but they don't agree. They say that he is only a satirist. Bentley is with his friend Wotton. He takes him by his side and onward they march looking here and there and making out some plan for the success. Bentley and Wotton go towards the camp of the Ancients. Their first adventure brings them upon the sleeping forms of Phalaris and Aesop. Bentley wants to kill them both. He aims his flais at Phalaris's breast but a goddess called Affright protects the Ancients from any harm, however, they steal their armous. Bentley leaving the two heroes asleep, goes in search of his dear friend Wotton.

Bentley roams here and there for a long time till he reaches a clear stream, called Helicon. He stops there and tries to drink the water. He tries times but everytime he fails. Then he stoops prove on his breast to drink its water. In the meantime Apollo comes there and holds his shield between the Modern and the fountain so that the Modern draws up nothing except mud. The reason is that Apollo begged of Jupiter, as a punishment to those who durst attempt to teste it with unhallowed lips, and for lesson to all not to draw too dep, or far from the spring.

It is then Bentley and Wotton happen to see Temple and Boyle by the fountain of Helicon where quite unaware of danger, these two Allies of the ancients were drinking deply of the limpid water. Wotton decides to kill the Destroyer (Temple). He grasps his lance and throws it towards Temple. Temple neither feels the weapon touch him nor hears it fall. Apollo is enraged. He orders boyle to take revenge. He (Boyle) advances against Wotton. He pursues Wotton and Bentley and transfixes both.

"Swift is clear but shallow

In originality and intellectual power, Jonathan Swift was by far the greatest writer of his time. To his contemporaries he was the formidable pamphleteer whose pen could endanger governments and discredit treaties. To many generations of children he has been the author of one of the most entrancing of fairy stories. To the lover of literature he is the satirist whose irony and intellectual power and rage are like forces of nature – tragic in their destructive might, uplifting in their exhibition of irresponsible power. **-Benrard Groom**

Swift is the most original writer of his time, and one of the greatest masters of English prose. Directness, vigour, simplicity, mark every page. Among writers of that age he stands almost alone in his disdain of literary effects. Keeping his object steadily before him, he drives straight on to the end, with a convincing power that has never been surpassed in our language. Even in his most grotesque creations, the reader never loses the sense of reality, of being present as an eye-witness of the most impossible events, so powerful and convincing in Swift's prose. Defoe had the same power; but in writing Robinson Crusoe, for instance, his task was comparatively easy, since his hero and his adventures were but natural; while Swift gives reality to pygmies, giants, and the most impossible situations, as easily as if he were writing of facts. Notwithstanding these excellent qualities, the ordinary reader will do well to confine himself to Gulliver's Travels and a book of well-chosen selections. For, it must be confessed, the bold of Swift's work is not wholesome reading. It is too terribly satiric and destructive; it emphasizes the faults and failings of humanity: and so runs counter to general course of our literature, which form Cynewulf to Tennyson follows the Ideal, as Merlin followed the Gleam, and is not satisfied till the hidden beauty of man's soul and the divine purpose of his struggle are manifest. Such is what Long says of him.

As a master of simple, direct, colloquial style-a style as far as possible removed from the ornate and the rhetorical – he has few rivals and no superior. His special field was satire and his favorite instrument irony, which is the art of swaying one thing in order to convey another. The skill with which, nominally adopting a position entirely alien from his own, he proceeds gravely and without once dropping the mask, to pour ridicule upon the very cause he is apparently supporting, is simply amazing. An excellent illustration will be found in his argument to prove that the abolishing of Christianity in England may ....be attended with some inconveniences, in which, writhing ostensibly as one who admits that ' the system of the gospel is generally antiquated and exploded', he makes a scathing attack both upon the free thinkers and upon the insincere professors of the current religion.

Sir I for Evans has rightly said that Jonathan Swift wrote, without regard for any man, vision of life as he saw it. The song list of satires extends from 'The Battle of the Book,' and 'a Tale of a Tub,' to 'Gulliver's Travels', and beyond, into the bitterer works of his last period. Swift has often been presented as a diseased misanthropist, who saw his fellow-men as the Yahoos of the fourth book of Gulliver. Little of this is true. Swift had a mind over-vexed by inconvenience and inadequacies of the physical appareatus of the human body, of its uncleanliness and its odours, and of the absurdity of the sexual act, when it is considered methodically by a non-participant. But his Journal to Stella shows that his fellow-men liked him and that to Esther Johnson, whom in many, if not all sense of the word he loved, he could show a genuine affection.

If Swift was arrogant in himself, he was modest in his philosophy, and would have man order his life without war, and without corruption, before he began more ambitious studies. It is typical of this modesty that his prose is clear, but it is a clarity sustained by the most vigorous mind of the century. It defies imitation. Never is the meaning obscure, and each argument is developed with a deadly certainty, not through rhetoric, but by putting the proper words in the proper places.

Swift's irony is the expression of proud, scornful temper, and of a critical mind of extreme lucidity. Much of his work is simply a refutation of the old maxim that human beings are endowed with reason. Looking at the religious and political divisions of the world, Swift saw that these were mostly about matters of secondary importance. The ultimate object of sound religion and good government were forgotten in the pursuit of minor ends.

The character of Swift's irony is unique. It consists in delivering an absurd remark, sometimes the exact opposite of his real meaning, with apparent seriousness. Often he is content with a few contemptuous sentences, as in his comment on the philosophers of Brobdingnag:

"After much debate, they concluded unanimously, that was only Relplum Scalcath,' which is interpreted literally, 'Lusus Nature', a determination exactly agreeable to the modern philosophy of Europe, whose professors, disdaining the old evasion of occult causes have invented this wonderful solution of all difficulties, to the unspeakable advancement of human knowledge."

The occasion of The Battle of the Books was a controversy between ancient and modern learning. The complexities of this dispute have long ceased to awaken much interest, and perhaps it is now chiefly remembered as having given rise to Swift's fable of the spider and the bee. The spider, which is the symbol of modern learning, does nothing but spin webs of sophistry form its own entrails, while the bee, who stands for the ancients, ranges far and wide over the fields, bringing back honey and wax, which provide men with the things they most need – Sweetness and Light.

Compton – Rickett observes that as a force in letters; Swift has impressed our own time more than he did his own. No Ironist save Defoe, or Fielding in Jonathan Wild, proved as clear and unequivocal as he : and Swift's irony, unlike theirs, glows tith consuming intensity of feeling. The words are like molten lead. Like other great stylists of the time Pope and Addison – he achieves a triumphant clarity; but unlike Pope he is never epigrammatic, unlike Addison he has little plasticity of form. He is plainly and forcefully clear, with a greater strength than theirs; all the more striking and cogent for his lack of ornament. There is no contemporary who impress one more by his marked sincerity and concentrated passion.

Swift's great value as a writer lies in his challenge to an easy, complacent optimism, and yet even here man is greater than his work. He remains a tragic and somber figure, reviling his age and crushed by it; an Ajax defying the lightning and smitten with blindness. Yet we realize his underlying greatness of genius the more clearly as we place him beside other writers of the time-Pope, Addison, Steele – and see how they dwindle in importance. For the issues he touched upon and the imagination he brought to bear upon them vastly transcended theirs. No finer thing has been said of his tragic life than was said by Thackeray : "To think of him is like thinking of the ruin of a great Empire."

Satire is a sort of glass wherein beholders do generally discover everybody's face but their own; which is the chief reason for that kind reception it meets with in the world and that so very few are offended with it. But, if it should happen otherwise, the danger is not great; and I have learned from long experience never to apprehend mischief from those understandings I have been able to provoke: for anger and fury, they add strength to the sinews of the body, yet are found to relax those of the mind, and to render all its efforts feeble and impotent.

There is a brain that will endure but one scrumming; let the owner gather it with discretion, and manage his little stock with husbandry; but, of all things, let him beware of bringing it under the lash of his letters, because that will make it all bubble up into impertinence, and he will find no new supply. Wit without knowledge being a short of cream, which gathers in a night to the top, and by a skill ul hand may be soon whipped into forth; but once scrummed away, what appears underneath will be fit for nothing but to be thrown to the hogs.

Against any case of hypocrisy or injustice Swift sets up a remedy of precisely the same kind, only more atrocious, and defends his plan with such seriousness that the satire overwhelms the reader with a sense of monstrous falsity. Thus his solemn argument to prove that the abolishing of Christianity may be attended with some inconveniences' is such a frightful satire upon the abuses of Christianity by its professed followers that it is impossible for us to say whether Swift intended to point out needed reforms or to satisfy his conscience or to perpetrate a joke on the Church, as he had done on poor Partridge. So also with his Modest Proposal', concerning the children of Ireland, which sets up the proposition that poor lrish farmers ought to raise children as dainties, to be eaten, like roast pigs, on the tables of prosperous Englishmen. In this most characteristic work it is impossible to find Swift or his motive. The injustice under which Ireland suffered, her perversity in raising large families to certain poverty, and the indifference of English politicians to her suffering and protests are all mercilessly portrayed.

Swift's two greatest satires are his 'Tale of a Tub' and 'Gulliver's Travels'. The Tale began as a grim exposure of the alleged weakness of three principal forms of religious belief, Catholic, Lutheran, and Calvinist, as opposed to the Anglican; but it ended in a satire upon all science and philosophy.

"Swift explains his whimsical title by the custom of mariners in throwing out a tub to s whale, in order to occupy the monster's attention and drivert it form an attack upon the ship, which only proves how little Swift knew of whales and sailors. But let that pass. His book is a tub thrown out to the enemies of Church and State of keep them occupied from further attacks or criticism; and the substance of the argument is that all churches, and indeed all religion, and science and statesmanship, are arrant hypocrisy. The best known part of the book is the allegory of the old man who died and left a coat (which is Christian Truth) th each of his three sons, Peter, Martin and Jack, with minute directions for its care and use. These three names stand for Catholics, Lutherans, Calvinists; and the way in which th3e sons evade their father's will and change the fashion of their garment is part of the bitter satire upon all religious sects. Though it professes to defend the Anglican Church, that institution fares perhaps worse than the others, for nothing is left to her – but a thin cloak of custom under which to hide her alleged hypocrisy."

In Gulliver's Travels the satire grows more unbearable. Strangely enough, this book, upon which Swift' literary fame generally rests, was not written from any literary motive, but rather as an outlet for author's own bitterness against fate and human society, it is still read with pleasure, as Robinson Crusoe is read, for the interesting adventures of the hero; and fortunately those who read it generally overlook its degrading influence and motive.

"Gulliver's Travel records the pretended four voyages of one Lamuel Guliver, and his adventures in four astounding countries. The first book tells of his voyage and shipwreck in Liliput, where the inhabitants are about as tell as one's thumb, and all their acts and motives are on the same dwarfish scale, in the petty quarrels of these dwarfs we are supposed to see the littleness of humanity. The statement who obtain place and favour by cutting monkey capers on the tight rope before their sovereign, and the two great parties, the Littlendians and Bigdndians and Bigendians who plunge the country into civil war over the momentous question of whether an egg sousd be broken on its big or its little end, are satires on the policies of Swift's own day and generation. The style is simple and convincing: the surprising situations and adventures are as absorbing as those of Defoe's masterpiece; and altogether it is the most interesting of Swift's satires.

On the second voyage Gulliver is abandoned in Broadingnag, where the inhabitants are giants, and everything is done upon an enormous scale. The meanness of humanity seems all the more detestable in view of the greatness of these superior beings. When Gulliver tells about his own people, their ambitions and wars and conquests, the giants can only wonder that such great venom could exist in such little insects.

In the third voyage Gulliver continues his adventures in Laputa, and this is a satire upon all the scientists and philosophers. Laputa is a flying island, held up in the air by a loadstone; and all the professsors of the famous academy at Lagads are of the same airy constitution. The philosopher who worked eight years to extract sunshine from cucumbers is typical of Swift's satiric treatment of all scientific problems. It is in this voyage that we hear of the Struldbrugs; a ghastly race of men who are doomed to live upon earth after losing hope and desire for life. The picture is all the more terrible in view of the last years of Swift's own life, in which he was compelled to live on, a burden to him self and his friends.

In these three voyages the evident purpose is a to trip off the veil of habits and custom, with which men deceive themselves, and show the crude vices of humanity as Swift fancies he sees them. In the fourth voyage the merciless satire is carried out to its logical conclusion. This brings us to the land of the Houyhnhnms, in which horses, superior and intelligent creatures, are the ruling animals. All our interest however, it centered on the Yakoos, a faithful race, having the form and appearance of men, but living in unspeakable degradation.

'The Battle of the Books' is a delightful fantasia – says Middlton Murray. The Battle of the Books is mainly in the form of a burlesque of Homer. Bentleyappears as a sort of Theorists, with Wotton as his young and beloved friend. Wotton if also the son and darling of the hideous goddess Criticism who is herself the offspring of Pride and ignorance. Her function in the battle is limited to helping Bentley and Wotton in vain. The conception of this goddess is based upon the first page of Temple's essay, where he says the occasion of his writing was his irritation at the complacency of two books praising modern writing at the expense of the classics.

'I could not read either of these strains without some indignation, which no quality in men is so apt to raise in me as sufficiency, the worst composition out of the pride and ignorance of mankind.'

'The hint for the famous episode of the bee and the spider which actually precipitates the battle of the books seems also to have come from a passage in Temple's essays. On poetry, in which he says that formal critical rules, such as that modern critics attempt to impose, are alien to the genius of poetry.

'The as if, to make excellent honey you should cut off the wings of your bees, confine them to their lives or their stands, and lay flowers before them such as you think the sweetest, and like to yield the finest extraction; you had as good pull out their stings and make arrant drones to them. They must range through fields as well as gardens, choose such flowers as they please and by proprieties and scents which they only can distinguish.

One more step – a big one, no doubt and the spider comes in as the symbol of criticism, atrabilious and enviously hostile to the free-ranging creativity represented by the bee.

"it is manifest that Swift's main purpose in The Battle of the Books is not to come to the rescue of Temple (who did not need it). And still less to make a contribution to the controversy (which had now become irrelevant to Temple's real's thesis), but to make fun of Wotton and Bentley and Dryden and anybody else who comes into his head – not wholly excluding Homer himself. Swift wants to enjoy himself, to give full rein to the vis comica bubbling up within him. Certainly, his sympathies, personal and rational, are with Temple; but his antipathies are much more decisive;. Against Bentley for his pedantry and bad manners against Wotton for daring to controvert Temple and to defend science against Dryden for telling him he would never be a npoet. But even these antipathies are not deadly; they are necessary to his creation. No one shoots well without a target.

Giving an account of the incident related in The Battle of the Books, Quinana has observed in his book, The Mind and the Art of Jonathan Swift. The Battle of the Books unlike A Tale of a Tub, is led in to by no bewildering maze of prefatory matter; there are only the notice of the bookseller to the reader and The Preface of the Author. The first sets forth concisely the origin of the dispute between Temple and his critics. The preface, but two paragraphs in length may seem to have a little relevance to what follows, but in fact it announces in paragraph two the chief theme upon which the ensuing satire is to be a series of variations.

There is a Brain that will endure but one scrumming. Let the owner gather it with Discretion, and manage his little stock with Husbandry, but of all things, let him beware of bringing it under the Lash of his Betters; because that will make it all bubble up into impertinence and he will find no new supply; wife, without knowledge, being a sort of Cream which gathers in a night to the Top and by a skilful Hand, may be soon whipt into forth, but once scumm'd away, what appears underneath will be fit for nothing but to be thrown to the Hogs.

The importunities of the early verse have vanished. We have instead a prime example of Swift's dolce still nuovo impertinence, defeating imagery, indirection, and implication. Wit without knowledge is a sort of Cream………….Thus is the revolt against reason indicated.

"In the body of the satire, the full and True Account of the Battle Fought Last Friday etc. – Five incidents may be distinguished. The first concerns the out-break of the quarrel among the books under Bentley's Care. Aside from the ingenuity displayed in investing the volumes with life and in neatly fitting the details of the allegory to the circumstances of the real quarrel, there is little that is remarkable here. The second incident is brilliantly handled..............upon the highest corner of a large Window there dwelt a certain Spider swollen upto the first Magnitude, by the Destruction of infinite, Numbers of Flies, whose Spoil lay scattered before the gates of his palace, like human Books before the cave of some Giant. Into the spider's web flies a bee, who extricates himself un harmed and pauses at a safe distance to clean his wings. The spider whose web has been ruined, spies the culprit and shouts insults at him: he is a rascal, a vagabond without house or home, living upn a universal plunder of nature. To which the bee replies at length; you boast that you are self-reliant, drawing and spinning out all from your self; That is to say, if we may jude of the Liquor in the vessel by what issues out, you possess a good plentiful store of dirt and poison in your Breast'..............'in short, the question comes all to this;

''Whether the noble being of the two, that which by a lazy contemplation of four inches round, by an over-weening pride, which feeding and engendering on itself, turns all into Excrement and venom; producing nothing at all, but Fly-bane and a cobweb, or that, which by a universal Range, with long srarch, much study, true Judgemnet and Distinction of things brings home Honey and Wax.

''Aesop overhears these recriminations and sums up the dispute. The Spider, with his love of dirt and his silf-sufficiency is a perfect modern; whereas the bee lives as do the ancients, bringing home honey and Wax and 'thus furnishing Mankind with the two noblest of things, which are sweetness and light;'

''Through out this incident the artistic economy is something to marvel at; there is not a superfluous phrase; from line to line the meaning is drawn out with a logical inevitability that makes of words the exact symbols of thought. As for the satiric effect, this is gained by means which the young versifier had understood but had not been able to manipulate, but over which the prose satirist has gained masterly control. The

Spider's every word and the entire series of images applied to him by the bee and by Aesop are nauseous. It is through disgust that Swift habitually attains his most forcible effect; all that is unacceptable to reasons is given an emotional repulsiveness so strong that it is attended by a definite visceral reaction. There is nothing quite comparable to Swift's mastery of disgust. Physical sensations of a different sort other writers have known how to arouse. Only Swift makes us reach at the irrational.

"The third incident includes the marshalling of the two hostile armies, the description of their respective leaders, the engagement of the two battle lines, and a number of hand-to-hand combats, wherein needless to say, the ancients are almost uniformly triumphant. Capital is the encounter between Virgil and Dryden. The former appears in shining armour astride a mettled horse. Towards him advances an unknown foe upon a sorrel Gelding of a monstrous size, old and lean whose high trot causes a terrible clashing of the rider's armour. The two cavaliers had now approached from within the throw of Lance, when the stranger desired a parley, and lifting up the vizard of his Helmet, a Face hardly appeared from within, which after a pause, was known for that of the renowned Dryden; A former heavy weight boxing champion is still remembered for his short punches : their power was crushing but they were delivered with such speed and at such short range that it took a slow motion camera to record them. When Swift chose he could hit like that. Only after we have found the pea inside the helmet and identified it as Dryden's head do we quite understand what has happened.

"The fourth incident splits the third. In the milky way the gods convened in council to watch the momentous battle now in progress on the library shelves Momus, patron god of the moderns, takes alarm at the impending fate of his children, and rushes for assistance to the goddess Criticism. This Deity.

'Had claws like a cat; Her Head and Ears and Voice, resembled those of an Ass. Her teeth fallen out before. Her eyes turned in-wards, as if she looks only upon her-self. Her diet was the overflowing of her own Gall; her spleen was so large as to stand prominent like a Dug of the first Rate, nor wanted Excrescencies in form of Teats, at which a Crew of ugly Monsters were greedily sucking.

"Concerned above all for her son Wotton, Criticism flies down to the scene of battle and in her own fashion encourages her children.

"The concluding incident impinges directly on Wotton and Bentley. Their past adventures on the field of battle recounted in mock heroic style are made to allegorize their attack on. Temple and their supposed defeat at the hands of Charies Boyle. Bravely the two moderns set out to raid the enemy, resolving by policy or surprise to attempt some neglected Quarter of the Ancients Army'. The picture they make as together they stalk their foes, only epic simile can give.

"As when two Mungrel curs, whom native greediness and domestic Want, provoke and join in partnership, though fearful, nightly to invade the folds of some rich Grazier; they with Tails depressed and lolling Tongues, creep soft and slow; meanwhile, the conscious Moon now in her zenith on their guilty Heads, darts perpendicular Rays, Nor dare they bard, though much provoked at her refulgent Visage whether seen in Puddle by Reflection or in Sphere direct, but one surveys the Region round, while t'other scouts the Plain...........so march'd this lovely, loving pair of Friends.

"Their first adventure brings them upon the sleeping forms of phalaris and Aesop, whose armour they steal – a goddess protects the ancients from further harm. It is then that they sight Temple, and Boyle by the fountain of Helicon where quite unaware of danger these two allies of the ancients are drinking deeply of the limpid water. Wotton darts his lance at Temple, but it falls harmless, whereas Boyle pursues the two marauders; let's fly a' Launce of wondrous Length and sharpness', and transfixes both.

"As, when a skilful Cook has truss'd a Brace of Woodcocks, He with Iron, Skewer, Pierces the etnder Spider of both their Legs and Wings close pinion'd to their Ribs; so was this pair of Friends transfix'd till down they fell, joyn'd in their Lives, joyn'd in their Deaths, so closely joyn'd that Charon would mistake them both for one and waft them over styx for half his Fare. Farewell, beloved loving pair; Few Equals have you left behind, and happy and immortal shall you be, if all my Wit and

Eloquence can make you." So ends this epic fragment, and with it The Battle of the Books.

The Champion of Reason in Style

Jonathan Swift is the most enigmatic and paradoxical figure among the greatest once of English literature. He has been praised by all critics old as well as modern. Dr. Johnson grudgingly spoke of his equable tenor of language which rather trickles than flows and his studied purity. Herbert Read praises his prose as narrative as direct and unobstructed as a fable. To him 'Swift's greatness consists in this fact, more than in anything else, that however deep his insight, his mode of expression remained simple, and clearly comprehensible.

This type of style flowed due to his dislike of all high flown ideals, his strong inclination for Reason which is imbedded in human nature, if only man is not perversely led away from it, in pursuve sickening ideals. With Dean Swift, prose is never an ornament, exercise, caper or complication of any sort. In most of his pronouncements on style, he has applauded 'simplicity which is one of the greatest perfections in any language'.

Swift's own views

'Proper words in proper places make the true definition of a style.' Swift was against 'the frequency of flat unnecessary epithets……….and threadbare phrases'. 'Beware of letting the pathetic part swallow up the rational.' He saw that 'passion should never prevail over reason.' And – A plain convincing reason may possible operate upon the mind both of a learned and ignorant hearer as long as they live, and will edify a thousand time more than the art of wetting the handkerchiefs of a whole congregation, if you were sure to attain it.

Ironical Vision

Swift's main instrument was not satire but unveiled irony in attacking contemporary shortcoming. It has been defined by Oxford Dictionary that expression of one's meaning by language of opposite or different tendency, especially stimulated adoption of another's point of view for purpose of ridicule. The Irony of Swift was not the product of any deliberate training in language but almost pathological as one may see from the candid letter he wrote to Alexander Pope, soon after finishing Gulliver's Travels (Sept. 29, 1725):

"I like the scheme of our meeting after distresses and dispersions; but the chief end I propose to myself in all my labors is to vex the world rather than divert it; and if I could compass that design, without hurting my own person or fortune, I would be the most indefatigable writer you have ever seenl, without reading .... but since you will now be so much better employed, when you think of the world give it one lash the more at my request. I have hated all nations, professions, and communities, and all my love toward individuals ; for instance, I hate the tribe of lawyers; but I love counselor such-a-one, and judge such-a-one : so with physicians – I will not, speak of my own trade – soldiers, English, Scotch, French, and the rest. But principally I hate and detest, that animal called man, although I hearty love John, Peter, Thomas, and so forth. This is the system upon which I have governed myself many years, but do not tell, and so I shall go on till I have done with them. I have got materials toward a treatise, proving the falsity of that definition, animal rationale, and to show it would be only rations capax."

By nature Swift was sensitive enough, as his friendships with Dr. John Arbuthnot, Viscount Bolingbroke, Pope and John Gay, demonstrate through the lines of the warmest letters ever written by man.

Society appeared to him – rightly enough, to be a collection of fervidities. He analyzed English society and politics from every angle – the professions, religious beliefs, political institutions, and habits and so on. Similarly the religious conflicts of the age are obliquely glanced at in his famous fling about where to break the Egg, at the big-end or the small-end. He fell frequently foul of politicians, the arma junta, the scientists and industrial promoters who began an era of exploitation. "Swift adopts a phraseology the out ward style, the manner of the humorist, but it is only to give intensity to the irony. Swift's irony was aimed against all the common failings of humanity, especially the pretentious nature of man. He could not help being bitterly ironical at the spiritualists' pursuit of inspiration :

"Too intense a contemplation is not the business of flesh and blood; it must, by the necessary course of things, in a little time let go its hold, and fall into matter. Lovers for the sake of celestial converse are but another sort of Platonics who pretend to see stars and heaven in ladies' eyes, and to look or think no lower; but the same pit is provided for both : and they seem a perfect moral to the story of that philosopher who, while his thoughts and eyes were fixed upon the constellations found himself seduced by his lower parts into a ditch."

"What in Swift is most important, the disturbing characteristic of his genius, is a peculiar emotional intensity." Remarks Prof. F. R. Leavis. Herbert Read comes to the same conclusion when he says, "Ironic wit such as Swift's even when engaged on the most trivial of subjects, is often a mask for deep feelings."

Satiric Prose

"There are two ends that men propose in writing satire, one of them less noble than the other, as regarding nothing further than personal malice; the other is a public spirit, prompting men of genius and virtue, to mend the world as far as they are able. And as both these ends are innocent, so the latter is highly commendable." Swifts satire is really of the second type. Like George Bernard Shaw and Aldous Huxley Swift also seized the dramatic situations which presented the discrepancies of life in a glaring light. "The role of his satire is therefore two-fold, first to catch the piquant situation and then to bring if forward into lime-light." In the On the Death of Swift (1731) he has deliberately paid a rich tribute to his satirical purpose:

Perhaps I may allow the Dean,

Had too much satire in his vein;

And seem'd determined not to starve it,

Because no age could more deserve it,

Yet malice never was his aim;

He lash'd the vice, but spared the name;

Not individual could resent,

Where thousands qually were meant;

His satire points at no defect,

But what all mortals may correct;

For he abhorr'd that senseless tribe

Who call it humour when they gibe.

He spared a himp, or crooked nose,

Whose owners set not up for beaux,

True genuine dullness moved his pity.

Unless it offer'd to be witty.

Those who their ignorance confest.

He ne'er offended with a jest;

He laugh'd to hear an idiot quote

A verse from Horace learn'd by rote.

His satires not only sought out ignorance and gullibility and lashed out against them but also singled out affections in speech and manners, in scholarship and the arts.

Swift is often fond of using offensive language at the height of his satirical fury. The happiest of Swift's satire is that exuberant work : The Battle of the Books.

"The books in St. James's Library get fed up with the quarrels and controversies among the scholars as to whether the Ancients are superior to the Moderns or vice versa. They begin to fight between themselves, that too only after exchange of embassies to thrash out the differences. These arise because the two factions in learning occupy 'two tops of the hill parnassus', the one occupied by the Moderns being slightly lower in height which make them put forward the impossible demand that the Ancient vacant their ancestral abode or reduce its attitude. The battle ensures in which the great leaders of both enter the lists for single combat.

'In this quarrel whole rivulets of ink have been exhausted and the virulence of both parties enormously augmented. Now, it must here be understood, that ink is the great missive weapon in all battles of the learned, which conveyed through a sort of engine called a quilt, infinite numbers of these are darted at the enemy, by the valiant on each side, with equal skill and violence, as if it were an engagement of porcupines.'

The satirical mockery reaches unprecedented heights when he describes the Moderns in battle array.

'The Moderns were in very warn debates upon the choice of their leaders; and nothing less than the fear impending from their enemies, could have kept them from mutinies upon this occasion. The difference was greatest among the horse, where every private trooper pretended to the chief command, from Tasso and Milton to Dryden and Withers. The light-horse were commanded by Cowley and Despreaux. There came the bowmen under there valiant leaders Descartes, Gassendi, and Hobbes, whose strength was such that they could shoot their arrows beyond the atmosphere, never to fall down again, but turn like that of Evander, into meteors, or, like the cannon-ball, into stars. Paracelsus brought a squadron of stink-pot flingers from the snowy mountains of Rhaetis.'

The most amusing satire is against Bentley the proud scholar, keeper of the Regal library at St. James's Palace : 'in person the most deformed of all the moderns; tall, but without shape or comeliness; large, but without strength or proportion.'

As a satiric artist, he finds his nearest rival only in Voltaire and also in Rabelais. Voltaire himself called Swift, 'Rabelais perfectionne.'

The Prose Style

Style is not an ornament; it is not an exercise, not a caper, nor complication of any sort. It is the sense of one's own self, the knowledge of what one wants to say and the saying of it in the most fitting words (Read and Dobree). Swift says-when a man's thoughts are clear, the properest words will generally offer themselves first, and his own judgment will direct him in what order to place them, so as they may be best understood. Where men arranges this method, it is usually on purpose, and to show their learning, their oratory, their politeness, or their knowledge of the world. In short, that simplicity, without which no human performance can arrive to any great perfection, is nowhere more eminently useful than in this.

Francis Jeffrey described Swift's style in these words: "It is radically a low and homely style without grace and without affection and chiefly remarkable for a great choice and profusion of common words no passion.

Swift prose is a reaction against the ornate emotional strain and decorative tendency of Sir Thomas Browne and the other writers of the Seventeenth century. His intention was to follow the path of commonsense and not that of fancy.

A selection of opinions of critics regarding the nature of his prose style shows a rare unanimity among them, ranging from Dr. Samual Johnson to Leslie Stephen, George Sainsbury and Elton. Here are a few select statements from writers on Style on Swift:

Dr. Samuel Jonson : "The rogue never hazards a metaphor His delight was in simplicity. That he has in his works no metaphor, as has been said, is not true; but his few metaphors seem to be received rather by necessity than choice. He studied purity...............His sentences are never too much dilated or contracted and it will not be easy to find any embarrassment in the complication of his clauses, any inconsequence in his connections, or abruptness in his transitions."

George Saintsbury : ''.................... there never, in English has been a prose in which harmony was secured with so few means taken to secure it, and monotony avoided with so little apparent effort to safeguard the avoidance."

G. A. Aitken : '' Swift's style is very near perfection clear, pointed, precise, he seems to have no difficulty in finding works to express exactly the impression which he wishes to convey...............There are no tricks of style, no recurring phrases, no ornaments, no studied effects; the object is attained without apparent efforts; with an outward gravity, masking the underlying satire or cynicism, and an apparent calmness, concealing bitter invective."

H. Craik : ''Of all English prose Swift's has the most flexibility, the most nervous of sinewy force; it is the most perfect as an instrument, and the most deadly in its unerring accuracy of aim."

Oliver Elton : '' In style, sculpture without beauty; in temper benevolence without love; mastery of intellect without serenity ....by stating these opposites we are not much closer than such a critic to a real divination of this mysterious figure whose artistic form is transparent and perfect, crowning the accomplishment of the purely prosew genius in English he stands apart from his environment, like an Agonistes of the older drama.

F.L. Lucas : '' Being what he was, he made a striking addintion to the infinite variety of the world; but one Swift seems to be quite enough. And his style is of interest as showing both what trenchancy the presence of imagery can give, and how much charm and colour its absence takes away."

The distinguishing features of Swift's Prose Style are :

(1) The use of imagery, (2) Serverity of diction and (3) Rhythm.

(1) '' For human life is a continual navigation, and if we expect our vessels to pass with safety through the waves and tempests of this fluctuating world, it is necessary to make a good provision of the flesh as seamen lay in store of beef for a long voyage."

(2) '' A soldier is a Yahoo hired to kill in cold blood as many of his own species, who have never offended him, as possibly he can.''

(3) '' For in Reason, all governed, is the very definition of slavery. But in fact, eleven men, well-armed will certainly subdue on singleman in his shirt.

So, Johathan Swift is undoubtedly the most forceful writer of prose in the History of Literature. He was born to write great prose just as Milton was born to compose Epic poetry'.

Gosses points out that The Battle of the Books was written to support Temple, who had been rather hard hit by Bentley and by William Wotton (1666-1726) in their Reflections upon Ancient and modern Learning. Swift, as in duty bound, is marshaled in the renks of the ancients' by Temple's side, and he makes shift to attack literary pretension in the person of a spider, whose castle 'it all built with my own hands, and the materials extracted altougether out of my own person.' The bee, the lover of qntiquity, is obliged to Heaven alone for my flights and my music.'

With our present views in criticism, it may seem that the Ancient should have been the spider and the Modern the bee, and Swift is very possibly laughing at his own allies in his sleeve. The narrative, which is what was then called a 'travesty', is supposed to be a 'full and true account of the battle fought last Friday between the ancient and modern books in St. James's library', of which Bentley was librarian, and we are to believe that the books themselves, being infected with the controversy raging outside, came to a decisive battle by flying at each other's heads; 'but the manuscript, by the injury of fortune or weather, being in several places imperfect', - a trick of composition which Swift loved to indulge in, ' we cannot learn to which side the victory fell.'

There has been litigation between those upper and lower peaks of Parnassus, on which the ancients and moderns respectively reside, and Bentley, a famous warrior among the latter, has vowed to compass the death of two valiant ancients, Phalaris and Aesop. He is baffled and retires to his library, where the books range themselves into two ranks and a new Trojan War br3eaks out, in which great advantage is gained to the ancients by the defection to their side of Temple who becomes their champion. Before the battle is described the apologue of the Spider and the Bee is introduced, illustrating allegory by still subtler allegory. When this is over Aesop rallies the ancients to the attack; they are gaining the day too easily when the horrible goddess Criticism in a chariot drawn by geese, arrives at St. James's and rushes into the fray in the guise of one of Bentley's pamphlets. The battle now becomes Homeric, and great heroes pluge into the fray on either hard; Aristotle lets an arrow fly at Bacon, but misses him and kills Descartes; Homer tramples Davenant in the dirt, and Virgil spears the life of Dryden, while the book closes with acquisitively diverting episode of Bentley and Wotton.

In the 1704 edition, The Battle of the Books was followed by the ironical fragment called The Mechanical Operation of the Spirit, an exposure of fanaticism which was to say the least indiscreet in the mouth of a young ecclesiastic eagerly ambitious to rise in the Church of England. Each of these treatises shows a great freedom from prejudice, a boundless impatience of humbug and pretension, and a savage touch which is all the more brutal because of the delicacy, keenness and power of sympathy, of which the author shows him inherently capable upon every page.

Fantasia is a fanciful musical composition. It is quaint, grotesque, extremely fanciful, and wild Burlesque is derived from Italian burla, ridicule, mockery, literary composition or dramatic representation which aims at exciting laughter by the comical treatment of a serious subject or the caricature of the spirit of serious word, Notable examples of burlesque in English literature are Butler's Hudibras, The Rehearsal, and Fielding's Tom Thumb.

Middleton Murray has observed that The Battle of Books is a delightful fantasia, mainly in the form of a buresque of Homer. Bentley appears as a sort of Thersites, with Wotton as his young and beloved friend. Wotton is also the son and darling of the hideous goddess, Criticism who is herself the offspring of

Pride and Ignorance. Her function in the battle is limited by helping Bentley and Wotton, in vain. The conception of this, goddess is based upon the first page of Temple's essay, where he says the occasion of his writing was his irritation at the complacency of two books praising modern writing at the expense of the classics.

"I could not read either of these strains without some indignation, which no quality in men is so apt to raise in me as sufficiency, the worst composition out of the pride and ignorance of mankind."

The hind for the famous episode of the bee the spider, which actually precipitate the battle of the books, seems also to have come from a passage in Temple's essay On Poetry, in which he says that formal critical rules, such as the modern critics attempt to impose, are alien to the genius of poetry.

'It's as if, to make excellent honey you should out off the wings of your bees, confine them to their hives on their stands, and lay flowers before them, such as you think the sweetest, and like to yield the finest extraction; you had as good pull out their stings and make arrant drones to them. They must range through fields as well as gardens, choose such flowers as they please and by proprieties and scents which they only can distinguish."

One more step a big one, no doubt – and the spider comes in as the symbol of criticism, atrabilious and enviously hostile to the free-ranging creativity represented by the bee.

It is manifest that Swift's main purpose in The Battle of the Books is not to come to the rescue of Temple (who did not need) and still less to make a contribution to the conspiracy (which had now become irrelevant to Temple's real thesis), but to make fun of Wotton and Bentley and Dryden and anybody else who comes into his head not wholly excluding Homer himself. Swift wants to enjoy himself, to give full rein to the Vis comica bubbling up within him. Certainly, his sympathies, personal and rational are with Temple; but his antipathies are much more decisive; against Bentley for his pedantry and bad manners, against

Wotton for daring to controvert Temple and to defend science, against Dryden for telling him he would never be a poet. But even these antipathies are not deadly; they are necessary to his creation No one shoots well without a target.

The Battle of the Books is a piece of satire marked with irony. There is only the notice of the bookseller to the reader and the Preface of the Author. It sets forth concisely the origin of the dispute between Temple and his critics. The Preface of the Author has only two paragraphs. In the second paragraph the author points out the chief theme o0f the satire of this book.

Satire is a sort of glass, wherein beholders do generally discover everybody's face but their own, which is the chief reason for that kind of reception it meets in the world and that so very few are offended with it. But if it should happen otherwise, the danger is not great, and, I have learned from long Experience, never to apprehend mischief from those understandings, I have been able to provoke; For, Anger and Fury, though they add strength to the sinews of the body, yet are found to relax those of the mind, and to render all its efforts feeble and impotent.

Theme, as proposed by Swift

There is a Brain that will endure but one scumming : let the owner gather it with Discretion, and manage his little stock with Husbandry; but of all things, let him beware of bringing it under the lash of his Betters; because, that will make it all bubble up into impertinence and he will find no new supply; wit, without knowledge, being a Sort of Cream, which gathers in a Night to the Top, and by a skilful Hand, may be soon whip into froth; but once scumm'd away, what appears underneath will be fit for nothing, but to be thrown to the Hogs.

Wit without knowledge is a sort of Cream...........Thus is revolt against reason indicated. In The Battle of Books five incidents may be distinguished. They are as follows –

The first incident

The first incident is concerned with the outbreak of the quarrel among the books under Bentley's care. Aside from the ingenuity displayed in investing the volumes with life and in neatly fitting the details of the allegory to the circumstance of the real quarrel, there is little that is remarkable here. " Whoever examines with due circumspection into the Annual Records of Time, will find it remarked, that War is the Child of Pride, and Pride the Daughter of Riches. – The former of which assertions may be soon granted; but one cannot so easily subscribe to the latter : For pride is nearly related to Beggary and Want, by Father or Mother, and sometimes by both; and to speak naturally, it very seldom happens among Men to fall out, when all have enough."

The second incident

The second incident is brilliantly handled...........upon the highest corner of a large window where dwelt a certain spider, swollen up to the First Magnitude, by the Destruction of infinite Number of Flies, whose spoils say scattered before the Gates of his Palace, like human Bones before the cave of some Glant. Into the spider's web flies a bee, who extricates himself unharmed and pauses at a safe distance to clean his wings. The spider whose web has been ruined, spies the culprit and shouts insults at him : he is a rascal, a vagabond without house or home, living upon a universal plunder of nature. To which the bee replies at length; you boast that you are self-reliant, drawing and spinning out all from yourself; "That is to say, if we may judge of the Liquor in the Vessel by what issues out, you possess a good plentiful store of Dirt and Poison in your Breast".............In brief, the question comes to all this-

"Whether is the nobler being of the two, that which by a lazy contemplation of four inches round, by an overweening pride, which feeding and engendering on itself, turns all into Excrement and Venom; producing nothing at all, but Fly – bane and a cobweb; or that, which by a universal Range, with long search, much study, true judgment and distinction of things brings home Honey and Wax.

Aesop wver hears there recriminations and sums up the dispute. The spider, with his love of dirt and his self-sufficiency is a perfect modern, whereas the bee lives as do the ancients, bringing home honey and wax and 'thus furnishing Mankind with the two Noblest of things, which are Sweetness and Light'.

Throughout this incident the artistic economy is something to marvel at; there is not a superfluous phrase; from line to line the meaning is drawn out with a logical inevitability that makes of words the exact symbols of thought. As for the satiric effect, this is gained by means which the young versifier had understood but had not been able to manipulate, but over which the prose satirist has gained masterly control. The spider's every word and the entire series of images applied to him by the bee and by Aesop are nauseous. It is through disgust that Swift habitually attains his most forcible effect; all that is unacceptable to reason is given an emotional repulsiveness so strong that it is attended by a definite visceral reaction. There is nothing quite comparable to Swift's mastery of disgust. Physical sensations of a different sort other writers have known how to arouse. Only Swift makes us reach at the irrational.

The third incident

The third incident includes the marshalling of the two hostile armies, the description of their respective leaders, the engagement of the two battle lines, and a number of hand-to-hand combats, wherein needless to say, the ancients are almost uniformly triumphant. Capital is the encounter between Virgil and Dryden. The former appears in shining armor astride a mottled horse. Towards him advances an unknown foe upon a sorrel Gelding of a monstrous size, old and lean whose high trot causes a terrible clashing of the rider's armour. The two cavaliers had now approached within the throw of Lance, when the stranger desired a parley, and lifting up the vizard of his Helmet, a Face hardly appeared from with, which after a pause, was known for that of the renowned Dryden. A former heavy weight boxing champion is still remembered for his short punches; their power was crushing but they were delivered with such speed and at such short range that it took a slow motion camera to record them.

When swift chose he could hit like that. Oney after we have found the pea inside the helmet and identified it as Dryden's head do we quite understand what has happened.

The fourth incident

The fourth incident splits the third. In the Milky way the gods are convened in council to watch the momentous battle now in progress on the library shelves. Momus, patron god of the moderns, takes alarm at the impending fate of his children and rushes for assistance to the goddess Criticism.

This deity 'had claws like a cat; Her head and Ears and voice, resembled those of an Ass; Her teeth fallen out before; Her eyes turned inwards, as if she looks only upon herself: Her Diet was the overflowing of her own Gall; her spleen was so large as to stand prominent like a Dug of the first Rate, nor wanted Excrescencies in form of Teats, at which a crew of ugly Monsters were greedily sucking.'

Concerned above all for her son Wotton, Criticism flies down to the scene of battle and in her own fashion encourages her children.

The last incident

The last incident impinges directly on Wotton and Bentley. Their past adventures on the field of battle recounted in mock – heroic style are made to allegorize their attack on Temple and their supposed defeat at the hands of Charles Boyle. Bravely the two moderns set out to raid the enemy, 'resolving by policy or surprise to attempt some neglected Quarter or the Ancients Army.' The picture they make as together they stalk their foes only epic simile can give.

''As when two Mungrel curs, whom native greediness and domestic want, provoke and join in partnership, though fearful, nightly to invade the Fold of some rich Grazier; they with Tails depress'd and lolling Tongues, creep soft and slow; meanwhile, the conscious Moon now in her Zenith, on their quality heads, darts perpendicular Rays; Nor dare they bark, though much provoked at her refulgent visage whether seen in Puddle by Reflexion or in sphere direct; but one surveys the Region round, while t' other scouts the Plan..........So march'd this lovely, loving Pair of Friends............."

Their first adventure brings them upon the sleaping forms of Phalaris and Aesop, whose armour they steal – a goddess protects the ancients from further harms. It is then that they sight Temple and Boyle by the foundation of Helicon where quite unaware of danger, these two allies to the ancients are drinking deeply of the limpid water. Wotton drats his lance at Temple, but if falls harmless, where as Boyle pursues the two marauders, lets fly a Lance of wondrous Length and sharpness, and transfixes both.

"As, when a skilful Cook has truss'd a Brace of Wood cocks, he with Iron skewer, Pierces the tender sides of both their Legs and Wings close pinion'd to their Lives, joyn'd in their Deaths; so closely joyn'd, that Charon would mistake them both for one and waft them over styx for half his Fare. Farewell, beloved, loving pair, Few Equals has you left behind; and happy and immortal shall you be, if all my Wit and Eloquence can make you."

Swift's prose style is of the plain and simple and kind, free of all affectation, and all superfluity, perspicuous, manly and pure. It is a plain style without ornament or embellishment and without forth or affectation. Swift delights in simplicity. It is remarkable for choice of common words and expressions precision is his aim and perspicuity his principal parise. His style is highly peculiar and characteristic. His penetration is great, his mode of reasoning clear, vigorous, attractive and convincing. His humour is perfectly his own. In the faculty of sarcastic humour Swift stands unsurpassed. "The Battle of the Books" an excellent piece of satirical humour.

Swift style conveys the impression of a tense energy but which commands and directs itself. It is controlled and disciplined. It is the most simple, vigorous and straight forward prose. His prose style has been held as the 'perfection of

English style.' It is a direct and forceful style marked by concentrated passion. Swift's manner is lyrical or impassioned. It is precise and colly controlled. Swift is master of conciseness.

"Ink is the great missive weapon in all the battles of the learned, which conveyed through a sort of engine called a quill, infinite numbers of these are darted at the enemy, by the valiant on each side, with equal skill and violence, as if it were an engagement or porcupines."

Swift is plainly and forcefully clear. He displays a triumphant clarity. He exhibits harmony without monotony. Swift's style is remarkable for its directness, vigour and simplicity. His mode of expression is simple and clearly comprehensible. Swift's style is convincing.

"For our horse are of our own breeding, our arms are of our own breeding, our arms of our own forging, and our clothes of our own cutting out and sewing."

Swift's style is concrete and homely. It is pointed and precise. There is poetic element in his style –

"I am glad, answered the bee, to hear you grant at least that I am come honestly by my wings and my voice, for then, it seems, I am obliged to Heaven alone for my fights and my music, and providence would never have bestowed on me two such gifts, without designing them for the noblest ends. I visit ....brings home and wax."

Swift's style contains flexibility. It suits varying moods. 'Farewell, beloved loving pair! Few equals have you left behind, and happy and immortal shall you be, if all my wit and eloquence can make you.'

Cazamian rightly remarks :

"Everything is clear in his style. It is bathed in ian intellectual light. Everywhere the language is that of reason itself, of a reason that is sensible to reality, nurtured by it and in no way abstract and dry. Swift knows how to employ the racy word, sometimes the coarse word, each word is in its place, quite naturally the fitting word is always chosen, without effort, though an instinct that seems spontaneous. A striking illustration of these remarks is found in the port royal of Bentley.

"His armour was patched up of a thousand incoherent pieces, ...his helmet was of old rusty iron............In his right hand he grasped a flail and (that he might never be unprovoked of an ffensive weapon) a vessel full of ordure in his left."

'The Battle of the Books' is a store house of sarcastic humour and irony. It reveals Swift master of sarcastic humour. The preface of the book provides evidence of his talent for sarcastic humour. In the opening paragraph of the book, he gives an example of sarcastic and ironical humour. He makes certain observations about what he calls the republic of dogs. The sarcasm or the irony lies in the fact that what is true of dogs is also true of human beings and of nations. They behave similarly.

The dispute between the Ancients and the moderns reveals 'Sarcastic humour. It is observed in the ridiculous behavior of the Moderns that they want to dislodge the Ancients from the higher summit. There is sarcastic humour in the description of the controversy between the two parties in which whole rivulets of ink were exhausted. Swift describes the funny behavior of the learned people. Sarcastic humour is observed in the description of Scotus and Aristotle joining. Together to dislodge Plato from the high position.

In the episode of the spider and the bee we observe sarcastic humour and irony in the self-parise of the Spider. His self-parise is his self-condemnation and there lies the irony. There is plenty of sarcastic and ironical humour in the mock-epic description of the armies and the battle. There is sarcastic humour and irony behind the portrayal of criticism. The actions of the goddess criticism reveal irony and sarcasm. Swift ridicules Dryden, Creech and Cowley. There is sarcastic humour in the manner in which Swift describes how venus changes one half of Cowley's dead body into a living done.

Swift makes an ironic portrayal of Bentley and Wotton. Sarcastic humour reaches its height when Scaliger says to Bentley : "

"The Malignity of thy temper perverteth nature; thy learning makes thee more barbarous; the study of humanity more in human, thy cornverse amongst poets more groveling, miry and dull."

The final words of farewell are sarcastic example of sneer at Bentley and Wotton –

"Farewell, beloved loving pair! Few equals have you left behind," etc. etc.

Thus, 'The Battle of the Books' is an excellent piece of satirical humour. In satirizing the modern and their absurdities, Swift makes use of irony and sarcasm to ridicule the moderns collectively and individually. Swift has made use of sarcastic and ironical humour as a weapon of Satire.

Numerical/analytical/Problematic Questions

The fable of the spider and the bee is Swift's real contribution to the debate between the Ancients and the Moderns. The analogy of the spider and the bee is both beautifully placed and beautifully carriedout. The episode is integral to the theme of 'The Battle of the Books.'

Swift describes the dispute between a spider (Moderns) and a bee (Ancients). Upon the highest corner of a large window there lived a certain spider. Into the spider's web flies a bee who extricates unharmed and pauses at a safe distance to clear its wings. The spider whose web has been ruined, spies the culprit and shouts insults at plunderer of nature. To which the bee assures to come near his kennel no more. He asks him to have patience.

The spider calls him rogue and advises him to respect his betters. The bee asks the spider why the thinks him superior to the bee. The spider curses the bee. He is born to no possession of his own except a pair of wings and a drone pipe. He is a plunderer and he steals honey from the garden whereas the (The spider) has been furnished with a native stock. He has his own castle to live in. he is rather a technician, a scientist than a foolish philosopher indulged in thinking and thinking.

The bee says that he (spider) dwells in a narrow space and feeds upon his own poison. He turns everything into poison by his excessive pride. He produces nothing useful. But on the other hand he (bee) produces boney and wax.

The episode of the bee and the spider is a piece of allegory. The episode is an ingenious device to illustrate the allegory by a still subtler allegory. The spider symbolizes the Moderns and the bee symbolizes the Ancients. It refers to the debate going on in England between the Champions of ancient learning and the champions of modern learning. Swift's 'The Battle of the Books' is in the form of an allegory. The books are depicted as warriors armed with various offensive and defensive weapons. It seems that the books belong to the two opposite parties actually attacking and causing salnghter. Within this allegory the episode of the spider and the bee is a briefer allegory. But then it intensifies and enlivens the main argument.

The episode nicely fits into the larger frame work. It is beautifully placed and beautifully worked out. The bee symbolizes Swift's ideal man of reason. He looks to objective experience. He produces honey and wax and through them the two nboblest things Sweetness and light. But the spider exhibits only artifloo and no real creativity.

"The Battle of the Books' is a mock-heroic in prose. It is a parody of an epic battle. It is a burlesque in prose of an epic. Its purpose is satirical. It refers to the controversy going on between the champions of ancient learning and the champions of modern learning. The battle was fought between the books written by ancient authors and books written by modern authors. The battle was fought on the shelves of the St. James's library. In this way Swift made fun of modern authors considered them inferior to ancient authors.

Swift employed he technique of mock epic He ridicules the champion of modern learning and made "The Battle of the Books" a parody or burlesque of an epic. He used devices accepted by the ancient epic poets. Homer and Virgil. Swift has depicted different stages of narration. He has showed books as armed warriors of different categories. He describes the successive encounters. The climax of the mock epic battle reaches in the final encounter in which Wotton and Bentley appear in a most unfavorable light. Boyle wins a decisive victory. The description of Bentley has been depicted in a mocking manner. The cowardice of Bentley and Wotton is satirized. At the end both are slain.

Swift makes use a few of other epic conventions in order to create comic effect. There is invocation to the muse of history. He uses supernatural machinery for a comic effect. He has put supernatural machinery to a satirical use. The intervention of gods and goddesses contributes to the mock-epic of 'The Battle of the Books.' Swift makes use of mock-epic similes to mock at Bentley and Wotton to degrade them. Apart from this Swift has made use of elevated language for a comic effect.

"His vehicle in the simpler 'The Battle of the Books' (out of respect of Bentley the battle took place in the royal library) is the prose mock heroic, and here Swift exhibits at its best the love of classical epic techniques that marked his period. The mock-epic simile in which Bentley and Wotton are spitted on a single spear and the episode of the spider and the bee, with the fine moral by Aesop, constitute perfection in new-classical writing."

The purpose of 'The Battle of the Books' is satirical. It ridicules and makes us laugh. It has excited laughter by the comical treatment of a serious subject. The book refers to the use of epic structure but on a miniature scale. It has dealt with a subject that is mean or trivial. It has revealed the atmosphere of mockery. Its object has been to ridicule modern authors and critics collectively and individually.

Swift mentions a number of authors – both ancient and modern – in his short satirical work 'The Battle of the Books.' The names of the ancient authors are – Phalaris, Aesop, Aristotle, Plato, Virgil, Homer, Pindar, Euclid, Herodotus, Livy, Hippocrates, Galen, Lucan and Horace. The names of the modern authors are Sir William Temple, William Wotton, Richard Bentley, Charles Boyle, Tasso, Milton, Dryden, Wither (Withers), Cowley, Despreaux, Descartes, Gassendi, Hobbes, Paracelsus, Harvey, Guicciardini, Davila, Polydore Virgil, Buchanan, Mariana, Camden, Regiomontanus Wilkins, Scotus, Aquinas, Bellarmine, L'Estrange, vossius (Voss), Bacon, Davenant, Denham, Wesley, Perrault, Fontenelle, Blackmore, Creech, Ogleby, Oldham, Mrs.Afra Behn, Scaliger, Aldro Vandus and Atterbury.

'The Battle of the Books' is a satire on modern authors. It is a satire on the Pedantry and the subjectivism of modern authors. It is an attack of destructive and negative criticism. It is a satire on mythological gods and goddesses also. It is a satire on the learned people who are intolerant of one another's point of view and make personal attacks upon one another.

'The Battle of the Books' is called a delightful fantasia. It is mainly in the form of a burlesque of Homer. Bentley appears as a sort of Thersites. Wotton is described as his yourn and beloved friend. He is also the son and darling of the hideous goddess criticism. She is the offspring of Pride and Ignorance. She helps Bentley and Wotton in vain. Swift pokes fun at Bentley and Wotton. It is a literary satire. Swift has written it as Sir William Temple declared his preference for the Ancient.

Swift is definitely and undoubtedly on the side of the Ancients. He stresses that the Ancients are more cultured than the Moderns. He praises the universality of the Ancients. They have exhibited the first hand experience of nature. They have provided sweetness and light to mankind.

The analogy of the bee and the spider is both beautifully placed beautifully carried out. The episode of the bee and the spider is an ingenious device to illustrate the allegory by a still subtler allegory. A bee (Ancients) flies into the web of a spider (Moderns) and ruins it. The spider shouts insults at him. He calls him a rascal, a vagabond, without home, a universal plunderer of nature. He advises him (bee) to respect his betters (spider). He (bee) has nothing except a pair of wings and a drone-pipe. He (bee) steals honey. But he has his own castle and he is a technician and a scientist. The bee says that he (spider) dwells in a narrow space and feeds upon his own poison. He turns everything into poison by his excessive pride. He produces nothing useful but on the other hand he produces honey and wax.

'The Battle of the Books' displays sarcastic humour and irony. There is sarcastic humour in the preface. The opening paragraph offers an example of Swift's sarcastic and ironical humour. He makes observations about what he calls the republic of dogs. What is true of dogs is also true of human beings and of nations. The dispute between the Ancients and the Moderns exhibits sarcastic humour. There is sarcastic humour and irony in spider's self-praise. It is seen in the portrayal of criticism also.

Swift's prose has been held as the 'perfection of English style. He is consummate in his skill clearness; directness and see arc most certainly the outstanding qualities of Swift's prose style. There is simplicity and clarity in it. It is a plain style. It contains force and vigous. It is precise and colly controlled. It has flexibility and conciseness.

'The Battle of the Books' is a mock-heroic in prose. It is a parody of the epic. A dignified style is used in it to deal with a trivial or mean subject. Swift describes books (or their authors) as fully armed warriors. They clash with one another in single combats like those described by Homer and Virgil in their epics (Iliad and Aeneid respectively). The description is in a tone of mock gravity. Swift also makes use of supernatural machinery for comic effect.

Swift uses supernatural machinery in 'The Battle of The Books' for comic effect. He has put supernatural machinery to a satirical use. The intervention gods and goddesses contributes to the mock-epic of 'The Battle of the Books'. Swift describes how in the Milky way the gods are in council to watch the momentous battle now in the progess on the library shelves. Momus patron god of the moderns, takes alarm at the impending fate of his children and rushes for assistance to the goddess criticism. This deity had claws like a cat. Her head and Ears and voice resembled those of an ass. Her teeth fallen out before. Her eyes turned inwards as if she looks only upon herself of her own gall. Her spleen like a Dug of the first Rate, nor a crew of ugly monsters were

Bibliography:

Connery, Brian A., ed. *Representations of Swift*. Newark: University of Delaware Press, 2002.

Ehrenpreis, Irvin. *Swift: The Man, His Works, and the Age.* 3 vols. Cambridge, Mass.: Harvard University Press, 1962-1983.

Quintana, Ricardo. *Swift: An Introduction.* New York: Oxford University Press, 1965.

Robinson, Elaine L. *Gulliver as Slave Trader: Racism Reviled by Jonathan Swift.* Jefferson, N.C.: McFarland, 2006.

Tuveson, Ernest Lee, ed. *Swift: A Collection of Critical Essays.* Englewood Cliffs, N.J.: Prentice-Hall, 1964.

Van Doren, Carl. *Swift.* New York: Viking Press, 1930.

Williams, Kathleen. *Swift: The Critical Heritage.* New York: Barnes & Noble Books, 1970.

Wood, Nigel, ed. *Jonathan Swift*. London: Longman, 1999.

Swift, Jonathan. *A Tale of a Tub and Other Works*. Marcus Walsh, editor. Cambridge: Cambridge University Press, 2010.

Stuart P. Sherman (1920). "Tale of a Tub, A, and The Battle of the Books". *Encyclopedia Americana*.

A Tale of a Tub, to which is Added the Battle of the Books and the Mechanical Operation of the Spirit, ed. A. C. Guthkelch and D. Nichol Smith (Oxford: Clarendon Press, 1920).

www.ingramcontent.com/pod-product-compliance
Ingram Content Group UK Ltd.
Pitfield, Milton Keynes, MK11 3LW, UK
UKHW051135260726
13967UKWH00010B/3058

9 781312 791343